EASY HOMEMADE RAW DOG FOOD RECIPES COOKBOOK

QUICK 25 EASY VET-APPROVED HOMEMADE MEALS FOR DOGS OF ALL AGES

Marry Williams

Contents

Introduction

"EASY HOMEMADE RAW DOG FOOD RECIPES COOKBOOK : is your go-to resource for crafting nutritious and balanced meals for your dog. From beginners to seasoned pet chefs, this guide provides a collection of recipes prioritizing your dog's health.

Raw Dog Food Diet:

Explore the benefits and considerations of a raw dog food diet, emphasizing uncooked, natural ingredients like raw meat, bones, fruits, and vegetables, mirroring the diet of wild ancestors.

Common Components in Raw Diets:

- Muscle Meat:Primary protein source for muscle health.

- Bones: Essential for minerals, dental benefits, and mental stimulation.

- Organ Meats: Rich in vitamins and minerals for a balanced profile.

- Fruits and Vegetables:Provide vital vitamins, fiber, and antioxidants.

- Supplements:Enhance skin, coat health, and address specific nutritional needs.

This book equips you with the knowledge to prepare nutritionally complete, homemade meals tailored to your dog's needs. Learn the essentials of raw feeding and ensure a happier, healthier life for your beloved canine companion.

Recipe 1. Beef and Quinoa Feast

Ingredients:
- 2 cups cooked and lean ground beef
- 1 cup cooked quinoa
- 1/2 cup finely chopped broccoli
- 1/4 cup blueberries
- 2 tablespoons flaxseed oil

Instructions:
1. Mix cooked beef, quinoa, chopped broccoli, and blueberries in a bowl.
2. Add flaxseed oil and stir until well combined.
3. Portion the mixture based on your dog's size and store as mentioned before.

Recipe 2. Salmon and Sweet Pea Delight

Ingredients:
- 2 cups cooked and flaked salmon (without bones)
- 1 cup cooked sweet peas
- 1/2 cup cooked brown rice
- 1/4 cup grated carrots
- 2 tablespoons coconut oil

Instructions:
1. Combine salmon, sweet peas, brown rice, and grated carrots in a bowl.
2. Add coconut oil and mix thoroughly.
3. Divide into portions and store accordingly.

Recipe 3. Turkey and Pumpkin Power Bowl

Ingredients:
- 2 cups cooked and ground turkey
- 1 cup cooked pumpkin puree
- 1/2 cup cooked green beans, chopped
- 1/4 cup cranberries (unsweetened)
- 2 tablespoons fish oil

Instructions:
1. Mix turkey, pumpkin puree, chopped green beans, and cranberries in a bowl.
2. Drizzle fish oil and stir well.
3. Portion and store as needed.

Recipe 4. Lamb and Barley Bliss

Ingredients:
- 2 cups cooked and diced lamb
- 1 cup cooked barley
- 1/2 cup cooked carrots, sliced
- 1/4 cup peas
- 2 tablespoons sunflower oil

Instructions:
1. Combine lamb, barley, sliced carrots, and peas in a bowl.
2. Add sunflower oil and mix thoroughly.
3. Portion and store in suitable containers.

Recipe 5. Veggie and Tofu Medley

Ingredients:
- 2 cups firm tofu, crumbled
- 1 cup cooked and diced sweet potatoes
- 1/2 cup cooked zucchini, diced
- 1/4 cup chopped parsley
- 2 tablespoons olive oil

Instructions:
1. Mix crumbled tofu, diced sweet potatoes, diced zucchini, and chopped parsley in a bowl.
2. Drizzle olive oil and toss until ingredients are evenly coated.
3. Divide into portions and store appropriately.

Recipe 6. Venison and Brown Rice Marvel

Ingredients:
- 2 cups cooked and shredded venison
- 1 cup cooked brown rice
- 1/2 cup cooked carrots, finely chopped
- 1/4 cup blueberries
- 2 tablespoons flaxseed oil

Instructions:
1. Combine shredded venison, brown rice, chopped carrots, and blueberries in a bowl.
2. Drizzle flaxseed oil and mix until well incorporated.
3. Portion and store as per your dog's requirements.

Recipe 7. Chicken Liver and Potato Potpourri

Ingredients:
- 2 cups cooked and finely chopped chicken liver
- 1 cup cooked and mashed sweet potatoes
- 1/2 cup green peas
- 1/4 cup chopped green beans
- 2 tablespoons coconut oil

Instructions:
1. Mix chopped chicken liver, mashed sweet potatoes, green peas, and chopped green beans in a bowl.
2. Add coconut oil and stir until thoroughly combined.
3. Divide into portions and store appropriately.

Recipe 8. Turkey and Lentil Bliss

Ingredients:
- 2 cups cooked ground turkey
- 1 cup cooked lentils
- 1/2 cup cooked carrots, grated
- 1/4 cup diced apples
- 2 tablespoons fish oil

Instructions:
1. Combine ground turkey, cooked lentils, grated carrots, and diced apples in a bowl.
2. Drizzle fish oil over the mixture and mix well.
3. Portion and store in suitable containers.

Recipe 9. Sardine Surprise

Ingredients:
- 2 cans of canned sardines in water, drained
- 1 cup cooked quinoa
- 1/2 cup cooked green beans, chopped
- 1/4 cup grated carrots
- 2 tablespoons olive oil

Instructions:
1. Mix drained sardines, cooked quinoa, chopped green beans, and grated carrots in a bowl.
2. Drizzle olive oil over the mixture and toss until evenly coated.
3. Divide into portions and store appropriately.

Recipe 10. Pork and Pumpkin Power Bowl

Ingredients:
- 2 cups cooked and diced pork
- 1 cup cooked pumpkin puree
- 1/2 cup cooked barley
- 1/4 cup cranberries (unsweetened)
- 2 tablespoons sunflower oil

Instructions:
1. Combine diced pork, pumpkin puree, cooked barley, and cranberries in a bowl.
2. Drizzle sunflower oil and mix thoroughly.
3. Portion and store as needed.

Recipe 11. Bison and Sweet Potato Stew

Ingredients:
- 2 cups cooked and shredded bison
- 1 cup cooked sweet potatoes, diced
- 1/2 cup green beans, finely chopped
- 1/4 cup blueberries
- 2 tablespoons coconut oil

Instructions:
1. Mix shredded bison, diced sweet potatoes, chopped green beans, and blueberries in a bowl.
2. Add coconut oil and stir until well combined.
3. Portion and store according to your dog's needs.

Recipe 12. Duck and Chickpea Extravaganza

Ingredients:
- 2 cups cooked and diced duck
- 1 cup cooked chickpeas
- 1/2 cup carrots, grated
- 1/4 cup peas
- 2 tablespoons fish oil

Instructions:
1. Combine diced duck, cooked chickpeas, grated carrots, and peas in a bowl.
2. Drizzle fish oil over the mixture and mix thoroughly.
3. Divide into portions and store appropriately.

Recipe 13. Turkey and Pumpkin Patties

Ingredients:
- 2 cups ground turkey, cooked
- 1 cup canned pumpkin puree
- 1/2 cup oats, finely ground
- 1/4 cup apples, diced
- 2 tablespoons olive oil

Instructions:
1. Mix cooked ground turkey, pumpkin puree, finely ground oats, and diced apples in a bowl.
2. Drizzle olive oil over the mixture and stir until well combined.
3. Form patties, portion, and store in the refrigerator or freezer.

Recipe 14. Haddock and Quinoa Crunch

Ingredients:
- 2 cups cooked and flaked haddock (without bones)
- 1 cup cooked quinoa
- 1/2 cup broccoli, finely chopped
- 1/4 cup raspberries
- 2 tablespoons flaxseed oil

Instructions:
1. Combine flaked haddock, cooked quinoa, chopped broccoli, and raspberries in a bowl.
2. Drizzle flaxseed oil over the mixture and toss until evenly coated.
3. Portion and store as per your dog's requirements.

Recipe 15. Lamb and Lentil Medley

Ingredients:
- 2 cups cooked and diced lamb
- 1 cup cooked lentils
- 1/2 cup sweet potatoes, diced
- 1/4 cup cranberries (unsweetened)
- 2 tablespoons sunflower oil

Instructions:
1. Mix diced lamb, cooked lentils, diced sweet potatoes, and cranberries in a bowl.
2. Drizzle sunflower oil and stir until well combined.
3. Divide into portions and store accordingly.

Recipe 16. Turkey and Barley Bake

Ingredients:
- 2 cups ground turkey, cooked
- 1 cup cooked barley
- 1/2 cup carrots, grated
- 1/4 cup blueberries
- 2 tablespoons coconut oil

Instructions:
1. Mix cooked ground turkey, cooked barley, grated carrots, and blueberries in a bowl.
2. Add coconut oil and stir until well combined.
3. Portion and store in suitable containers.

Recipe 17. Kangaroo and Quinoa Surprise

Ingredients:
- 2 cups cooked and shredded kangaroo meat
- 1 cup cooked quinoa
- 1/2 cup peas
- 1/4 cup diced apples
- 2 tablespoons fish oil

Instructions:
1. Combine shredded kangaroo meat, cooked quinoa, peas, and diced apples in a bowl.
2. Drizzle fish oil over the mixture and mix thoroughly.
3. Divide into portions and store appropriately.

Recipe 18. Venison and Potato Potluck

Ingredients:
- 2 cups cooked and diced venison
- 1 cup sweet potatoes, mashed
- 1/2 cup green beans, finely chopped
- 1/4 cup cranberries (unsweetened)
- 2 tablespoons olive oil

Instructions:
1. Mix diced venison, mashed sweet potatoes, chopped green beans, and cranberries in a bowl.
2. Drizzle olive oil over the mixture and toss until evenly coated.
3. Portion and store as per your dog's needs.

Recipe 19. Tilapia and Brown Rice Fiesta

Ingredients:
- 2 cups cooked and flaked tilapia (without bones)
- 1 cup cooked brown rice
- 1/2 cup carrots, grated
- 1/4 cup peas
- 2 tablespoons flaxseed oil

Instructions:
1. Combine flaked tilapia, cooked brown rice, grated carrots, and peas in a bowl.
2. Drizzle flaxseed oil over the mixture and toss until well combined.
3. Portion and store in suitable containers.

Recipe 20. Pork and Pumpkin Pleasure

Ingredients:
- 2 cups cooked and diced pork
- 1 cup canned pumpkin puree
- 1/2 cup cooked barley
- 1/4 cup raspberries
- 2 tablespoons sunflower oil

Instructions:
1. Mix diced pork, pumpkin puree, cooked barley, and raspberries in a bowl.
2. Drizzle sunflower oil and stir until thoroughly combined.
3. Divide into portions and store accordingly.

Recipe 21. Chicken and Chickpea Fiesta

Ingredients:
- 2 cups cooked and shredded chicken (boneless, skinless)
- 1 cup cooked chickpeas
- 1/2 cup sweet potatoes, diced
- 1/4 cup blueberries
- 2 tablespoons coconut oil

Instructions:
1. Mix shredded chicken, cooked chickpeas, diced sweet potatoes, and blueberries in a bowl.
2. Add coconut oil and stir until well combined.
3. Portion and store in airtight containers.

Recipe 22. Beef and Pumpkin Pleaser

Ingredients:
- 2 cups lean ground beef, cooked
- 1 cup canned pumpkin puree
- 1/2 cup green beans, finely chopped
- 1/4 cup diced apples
- 2 tablespoons fish oil

Instructions:
1. Combine cooked ground beef, pumpkin puree, chopped green beans, and diced apples in a bowl.
2. Drizzle fish oil over the mixture and mix thoroughly.
3. Divide into portions and store appropriately.

Recipe 23. Quail and Quinoa Quotient

Ingredients:
- 2 cups cooked and shredded quail meat
- 1 cup cooked quinoa
- 1/2 cup carrots, grated
- 1/4 cup peas
- 2 tablespoons olive oil

Instructions:
1. Mix shredded quail meat, cooked quinoa, grated carrots, and peas in a bowl.
2. Drizzle olive oil over the mixture and toss until evenly coated.
3. Portion and store as per your dog's requirements.

Recipe 24. Lamb and Lentil Love

Ingredients:
- 2 cups cooked and diced lamb
- 1 cup cooked lentils
- 1/2 cup sweet potatoes, mashed
- 1/4 cup cranberries (unsweetened)
- 2 tablespoons sunflower oil

Instructions:
1. Combine diced lamb, cooked lentils, mashed sweet potatoes, and cranberries in a bowl.
2. Drizzle sunflower oil and stir until well combined.
3. Divide into portions and store accordingly.

Recipe 25. Bison and Barley Bonanza

Ingredients:
- 2 cups cooked and shredded bison
- 1 cup cooked barley
- 1/2 cup carrots, finely chopped
- 1/4 cup raspberries
- 2 tablespoons flaxseed oil

Instructions:
1. Mix shredded bison, cooked barley, chopped carrots, and raspberries in a bowl.
2. Add flaxseed oil and stir until well combined.
3. Portion and store in suitable containers.

<u>Recipe Tracker</u>

<u>Guide</u>

Week Days	Daily Recipes	Remarks
Day 1		
Day 2		
Day 3		
Day 4		
Day 5		
Day 6		

Day 7		
Day 8		
Day 9		
Day 10		
Day 11		
Day 12		
Day 13		
Day 14		
Day 15		

Happy cooking

www.ingramcontent.com/pod-product-compliance
Lightning Source LLC
Chambersburg PA
CBHW040317240726
48664CB00006B/1521